Books by
Beclee Newcomer Wilson

Woman in Bits and Pieces
Tassajara Wind

Winter Fruit

Beclee Newcomer Wilson

Library of Congress Control Number: 2011908367
ISBN: Hardcover   978-1-4628-7596-2
                Softcover   978-1-4628-7595-5
                Ebook   978-1-4628-7597-9

This book was printed in the United States of America.

Cover and Interior by Beclee Newcomer Wilson

To order additional copies of this book, contact:
Xlibris Corporation
1-888-795-4274
www.Xlibris.com
Orders@Xlibris.com
98718

For John

For all the seasons we've shared

I would like to thank my colleagues in the Napa Valley College poetry class, led by poet George Stratton. Jane Hirshfield, Brenda Hillman, Elizabeth Alexander, and Arthur Sze, my teachers in the Napa Valley Writers' Conference.

Bonnie Long and Jennifer Nichols, companion poets with valued insights. Barbara Chambers, Joan Westgate, Anne Hamilton, Pat Friday, and Rebecca Kuiken—friends who share my love of poetry.

Beth Anne Wilson, Marcello Estevão, and Ian, Nate, Rebecca Estevão, Ben Wilson, Sandy Pfaff, and Gabriel Wilson, whose love surrounds my poems.

Beclee Wilson is the author of two previous collections of poetry: *Woman in Bits and Pieces* and *Tassajara Wind*. A graduate of Northwestern University, with an M.A. from the University of Michigan, and a Ph.D. from the University of Minnesota, poetry has always woven itself through her personal and career pursuits. She has studied with Jane Hirshfield, Brenda Hillman, Elizabeth Alexander, and Arthur Sze at the Napa Valley Writers' Conference. Beclee has also taught poetry in the Saint Helena Elementary School. She lives with her husband in the Napa Valley, of California, where gardening, growing grapes, painting, and writing fill her days.

Winter Fruit is a collection poems—intimate and accessible, deep and touched with a soft irony. Beclee Wilson places life experience, nature, and the writing of poetry under a magnifying glass and ponders what nourishes. There is a harvest to be gathered from these poems—a way to wisdom and endurance made accessible by a wise woman.

> There are times words
> create impression
> a sort of permanence
> out of fragile existence . . .

Like "marks in thin graphic strokes," Beclee Wilson composes a moving suite of elegiac poems attuned to empty spaces, to love, to the passage of time, and to what endures.

Arthur Sze

A sweetness runs through these quiet poems—sadness and the color of a garden, of a river rippling by, of oak leaves and tree lichen. Things that are true, that last, that pass away: "secrets too good to shout."

Norman Fischer

Contents

Winter Fruit

Markings

Dan left his book of poems
open on my coffee table.
There are marks in thin graphic strokes
by some titles in the Contents.

I go to empty spaces
poems without markings
no trace of visitation.
Did he stop by these
settle in for a stanza
then move on leaving no trace?
Had he meant to leave a mark?
An oversight perhaps
something left for returning.

A book of poems is best like this:
some verse for grasping
others for passing by with the intention
to visit another time—no order to follow
more like meandering a beach at sunset
or wandering through wildflowers,

traveling between covers
no thought of getting somewhere
no linear order needed to follow a plot.
Some touch you and there's a mark
left to find your way back.
Sometimes there's a title
noted by empty space
waiting to be explored.

Bare Roots

Today we planted eight blueberry bushes.

I cleared the plot of weeds. You dug holes,
breaking up hidden clay, moving rocks tucked deep.
Each slice and thud of the shovel showed
how strong you still are.

Bare roots are such spindly starts.
Seems hardly worth the effort,
this reality now in a staggered
line along the wall.

Well, imagine a summer morning
picking plump blue-purple
beads dusted in white blush
right off our own bushes!

Brix*

I search for purple sweetness on the vine,
slash leaves, tight clusters cut then toss away.
Spray off the mist the fog has left behind,
pierce fruit, at times before a hint of day.
I test for brix—select the harvest's best.
In all grapes left, sweetness is on the rise.
And now a humble task before I rest.
How quick the blade that strips away the prize.
If longings in my heart could be pierced so,
and Cupid's arrow touch a love that's true.
Then all the bleeding longing that would flow
could blend a treasured vintage shared with you.
Come! Sit with me! Taste our sweet time made strong.
This harvest like our grapes may soon be gone.

* The test to determine wine grapes' readiness for harvest

Having Second Thoughts

Perhaps
if I had pruned
early
the stems
would not be so stiff
unyielding in my blades,
left with gray-brown amputations.

I take away seeds
the yellow finches crave.
They make staccato movements,
signal their presence in the
long streaks of afternoon sun.

Well, I have no regrets.

There's a cycle
bloom and fade.
Time twists,
buds
become
compost.

Couples

We separate
in a show of independence,
I to my garden, you to practice piano.

Knowing though we go our separate ways
we travel inside each other
closer than the pause between each breath.

Turkey vultures twist above in solitary circles,
butterflies rarely flit in pairs.
They find each other.

Brix Reprise

Balance of sugar and acid
measure ripeness,
determine the moment of harvest.

Positioned to intercept light
leaves closest to clusters
produce the most sugar.

In moonlight,
tucked in your arm,
rising on each breath,
dreams are sweet

A Musing

I
Even though my world is not perfect,
I have daffodils for companions.
For breakfast, oranges
picked from my own trees.
Beyond the wooden fence
two fawns frolic
in touch with morning
touching their coats.

II
I keep struggling, wishing
I could tidy up a few traits
prune here, dig out there.
When beyond the perfect
part of the garden
there's a plot I leave alone,
let decide what will grow.
It always gives me surprises.

III
Birds catch
ascending heat
draw circles when they're
bored with straight-line flight.
Heights make me dizzy.
I knife my spade deeper
protecting from frost
that could ice my heart.

Reunion

The Gasconade River
bolt of amber satin
ripples by sycamore,
hickory, oak.

Leaves drift
in current patterns
gold and rust brown.

You walk the road
imagine your long-ago
canoe shoving
off from shore.

Lying in grass
I watch a trailing
spider web
travel on wind breath.

Wait for a man
searching for
a boy.

Between the desire
   To go forward, or go back
      Like squirrels on the road

Conversations Caught
in the Coffee House

I'm eavesdropping, people watching—
an old woman frowns into the Arts Section
of the *New York Times*, turns to neighbor,

"You look like Shawn Adams."
"No, I'm his brother. He's in L.A.
taking a break from medical school
trying to be an actor. Don't know
what got into him."

The man in the chair behind me remarks,
"I'm heading to Florida. Snorkeling for scallops.
Ya know they can swim!"

Writer by the window, mirrors me.
He composes, eyes darting for content,
I troll for inspiration—

fish with a pen, a journal, and coffee.
Latching on to the conversation of strangers.
Someday, I'll be the old woman
staring into the *Times*.

Coffee House Tempo

Break the croissant
in a shower of flakes.
Hold the cup,

warm fingers in white ring.
Lean close now
in a circle
all hushed tones.

Everyone
has secrets
too good to shout.

Only Half the Picture

It's okay.
She understands. It's him.
The tie, the purple Italian silk tie,
the sexy un-shaven look.
Fans like it. It scratches her.

The casual cut of his gray cashmere
jacket—gorgeous!
They waffled over the matching
purple handkerchief,
decided no.

Hours, she spent dressing,
torn between the lavender chiffon
strapless with the matching bag and
the silver shoes, or more her,
the demure cream crepe
with spaghetti straps, accentuated
by the dangling pearls. (His wedding
anniversary gift last year.)

Wasted energy.
Only half of her appears
on the opening night . . .
And the caption reads:
"Francis Ford Coppola
with unknown woman."

Degrees of Learning

Rolling my red lettuce leaves
in a blue and white tea towel,
laying them aside in the cool
of the " ice box", I think about
Carolyn, who taught me.
We were fat, with bellies holding
daughters who now hold their own.
Did Faith Baldwin, writing secrets
in *Family Circle*, teach her?
So much academe neglected,
like perfect biscuit making,
technique for turkey basting.
Not that we aren't wiser having
diplomas with full names
traced in raised gold
hanging on family room walls.
We have our "incidental learning" degrees,
legacy of the never to be forgotten
gathered from the everyday.
Collection of bird and plant names
learned on picnics. Camping
nights sleeping on a mountain pass
under Milky Way, Orion, after Venus
inscribed herself on the twilight sky.

Frequent-Flyer Miles

Seat 12f

I find I prefer to sit
window-view, watch hints
of fields in straight-edged patches.
Iowa, I believe.

I like my own company.
Chatting with strangers
requires a neck twist
hardly worth the illusion
of a new lifelong friendship

promises we'll always sit together
in 12f and 12e
no matter the flight.
Pick up where we left off
complete our story.

Conversation is too much effort
when already there's so much company
and look, isn't that a curve
of the Mississippi
just below?

Eating the Leftovers

seaweed that came with the sushi
      the last edge of warm
Point Reyes blue spread
       on progressively stale baguette

cooled candle drippings
      the Neil Simon CD

        cabernet, down to the dregs
your fragrance
      tie
       blue shirt
         tweed jacket—always too warm
      for California, you said.

diminishing sound on the gravel

      the red eye of your tail light

Writing

Words like fences
like long-branched
straight lines of trees

Allée for thoughts
moving in and out
searching for a voice

Scraps

There are times
>>> words create impression

a sort of permanence
>>> out of fragile existence

Like holding a butterfly
>>> on an open hand

ink rests on paper

thoughts   start traveling

Throw Away

Soft gray sky,
signature of summer fog . . . w he r . . .
All I can write
Ball point dried

I used to dip
into an inky
blue-black sea
pull back the metal clip
listen to gurgling
sucking sound
word surge
ponderings
impressions
purpose
persuasion
agony
sensuous and steamy . . .
all scripted through a gold wedge.

Fountain pens could dream!

Bloodline

Chocolate brown eyes
race along
gathering words
for the first time.
Like fruit picked in an orchard,
like nuts gathered from the ground.

Was it she who wrote
in the front of this leather book—
gold gilt still bright ?
Reading through unknown lands,
was she carried to adventure
of her own?

I see her leaning on a steel railing
listening to the piercing steamer whistle,
waving a white embroidered handkerchief,
her catcher of wind,
leaving behind on receding waves
all that's familiar all that says home.

This ancestor is in me
flowing through genetic code
watching my thoughts
travel across this page.

Choosing a New Journal

I'm moving away from black
covered sketch books.
Before me, varying sizes
colorful covers
lined or unlined paper
heavy artistic quality
for drawing and words.

They all scream
anarchy of choice!

I come to their level
sit cross-legged
on the bookstore floor
like I'm at Scout camp.

But, it's not camp,
I'm examining journals.

The one with the fine
ink drawing
of a Dragon Fly
spine of dizzy black spirals
seems ready to hold thoughts.

No Separation

What does the poet know,
following me around like she does!

Plumbing for words,
looking through my eyes,
naming *cardinal*, with its

scarlet flutter hiding in
ornamental pear
whose roots push
brick beneath my feet.

We exchange phrases, she and I.
Select and discard metaphors

until simple said, roots swell.
All walking requires
watching your step!

Poet's Muse

He searches the crowd
at the cocktail hour.

Presses his lip
on the wine glass rim.

She moves just close enough
to brush his arm

red lips parted, a hint of a smile.
For a night, or two, she will

breathe into him
fire he cannot ignite alone.

Keepsake

A book without lines
  Nothing keeps my thoughts straight
    Flowers pressed on page

Flowers pressed on green
  Lines drawn for lost stems
    Remembrance of first spring

Remembrance of our Spring
  Soothes the pain of leaving
    Loss springs from the page

Traces along the page
  Faint fragrance lingers
    On dried blossoms

Umbrella opens
    Protection from wind and rain
        Nothing hides my tears

Pieces

There are times

reality   shatters

mirror shards
                    jumble   clarity

Thoughts echo

            through heart canyons

searching out familiar territory

Waiting Rooms

Sitting here in irregular time
palpitations of unexpected outcomes
mimic a heartbeat rhythm
in syncopated cadence.
I have nothing to make into rhyme.
Life ticks in stretched-out hours
on uncomfortable chairs
gathered in rigid squares
holding people with blank stares
turning pages of outdated magazines
names and addresses ripped off.

Suspended existence lies
behind the pull of a cotton curtain.
No audience, just empty space
between the anticipations of life.
No words dance in spectacular twists
no clever turn of phrase congregates
near gurneys describing
the other waiting one
in the open-back gown
watching the rhythm in the ECG.

Poetry skips these unpleasant pauses,
these waiting times
in waiting rooms.

Lament

My old loves are dying.

Lost, the soft shelter of the unrequited.
Imagined moments consummating
small intimacies now live only in dreams.

I wish I'd gone first,

watched them at *my* wake, in tears,
choked on remembered moments—
all they had kept from me,
all they locked from themselves.

I imagine them flushed from recurring longings
turning to complete strangers as they
sip chardonnay, hold smoked salmon

on toast rounds, in a napkin
with my initials, in silver, declaring,
"She was the love of my life."

Too late, too late, the old flame guttered.

Memoriam

wind wail
  rain slash
    wave tumble

rush to fill the void
  silence holds
    emptiness
      that feels so full

in time
  remembered walks
    shared dip of oar
      turn of phrase
        bring him back

Postmortem

Bear with me
while I pause
on the outskirts of emotion.

Hold my breath
like a cupped leaf on water
float or sink,

a deer frozen
on the road
statue of indecision.

You know what I mean
move on, go back
knowing each tremor

makes the rift
deeper, no clearer
only more pain.

Stand by me,
I'm walking with tears
to the center of sorrow.

Spoilers

Black mission figs
ripen inside branches.

Stellar jays
slash purple flesh
open seedy wounds.

Spoilers always
find a way-
leave a trace.

A Changing Heart

I pinch
roses from stems

reveal small buds
fresh
not quite open

Pinching
fear places
brings tears

makes room
to grow
untangled

You'll find me
wrapped in tissue
tied in raffia

Open

Flotsam and Jetsam
Japan 2011

small boy beats stones in
rhythm to quell his fear
world stretches and tips
axis pouring water bringing fear

To hell with the wind?
Confound the rain!
I recognize no Buddha.
A blow like the stroke of lightning—
A world turns on its hinge.*

what is to fill empty cubicle
on my calendar, fear?
time moved outside the box
only a slice of yesterday appears

A water bird, asleep
floats on the river
between life and death.*

small girl given comfort by
a mother who cannot cry tears
refusing to cry salt when
all below the hill salt brings tears

Not even in a moment
do things stand still—witness
color in the trees*

the car on the house, the ship on the road
how will they disappear
how can the tide so far away
have come so near

And won't there be
a teahouse among the cherry blossoms
along the way of death?*

no fear no tear no question
only flotsam and jetsam

* *Japanese Death Poems*, Charles E. Tuttle Co.

Condolence

The paper is smooth
satin to the touch.
My pen poised
to say something
of condolence.

Outside, gray sky
pitches tight crystals
tapping pavement.
First daffodils
yellow cups on petal saucers
bend like the bare branches
barely holding buds.

I think of my friend
at a loss
like my pen
pausing wondering
what will flow
out of emptiness.

Frost on grape vine buds
　Valley fans begin blowing
　Angry buzzing bees

Trying to Capture October

My basket holds
fat tomatoes
last-born of my harvest

Squash that hid among
leaf tangles
like eggs

Cricket songs
soprano whistles
calling to early evening

Stars hung in blue-black
not shuttered by street light

Curve of moon
soon so full
with autumn abundance

I pretend
nothing will change
even though harvest means
slashing grapes from vines

And part of me
writing dates on pages
impatiently awaits winter fruit

Local Landscape

Morning mist softens
brittle amber grass
thirsty for rain.

Oak moss tendrils
tight on branches
sway like tossing hair.

Tree lichen stiff
in summer shades of gray
turn celadon, soft to touch.

Only plunking acorns
break the hush.

Prelude to Winter

Today a green stream flows on the meadow—
brilliance of first shoots emerging
from a mat of limp tan grass to
surrender in first rain. It's neon now,
needing shades to shield the dazzle.
This California valley, this outrageous
everywhere of winter green
upsets sensibility born in a somber season
waiting for snow to bury any hint of new life.
Here water of winter impresses connection
mingles farewell and welcome
denies separation of death and birth.
All along this streaming of emerald
my shoeprints bow the new arrivals.

Through spring and summer
Blue Oak leaves hold in stiff clusters
hardly a dip in the breeze
tolerant of heat, quiet and dreamlike
through warm nights and dewless dawn.
Today in castanet-clicking and dervish whirls
they give a farewell wave. Gusts hint of storm,
leave stark branches tracing across a sky
heaped in charcoal-edged clouds.
Sun peeks, now and then,
through a gauzy shroud.
Soft yellow rays change windows
catching their first southern exposure.

Twilight Stony Hill Road

Sun slides behind hill
pulls apricot and rose
off grass and vines
flings it into the sky.

It's called alpenglow.

Breeze holds its breath
listens for raspy
wing beat of crows.
Along the road
trees no longer drink.

Creek runs full.

Spider Span

On my morning walk
I cross the bridge
at the mill

walk through a spider span
silky touch and tickle—

bridge to travel
from one place to another

Snapping connections
from home gives
freedom for adventure

Artemis Dreaming

Under full moon
On soft padded paws
Lion circles the fire
Velvet balls swaying
Night holds lightning flashes

His fingers trace my contours
Learn the rifts and valleys
Dark moist places
Plateaus parched and dry

I gather persimmons
Winter-stored sun
Clings on branches
Clings longer than leaves
Longs to suck the last warmth

I gather pomegranates
Crown torn
Pulled open
Seeds plucked from crevices
Dripping blue-red juice

Arms encircling me, mine
Gently rocking
Fingering lace
Under full moon

Crystals

These will not be poems for you.
So I will call them crystals
thoughts and feelings
forming under great pressure.

These will not be poems for you.
So I will call them vapors
condensing on the surface
when the air chills.

These will not be poems for you.
So I will call them bits
and pieces of life visible
after all the rest of us moved on.

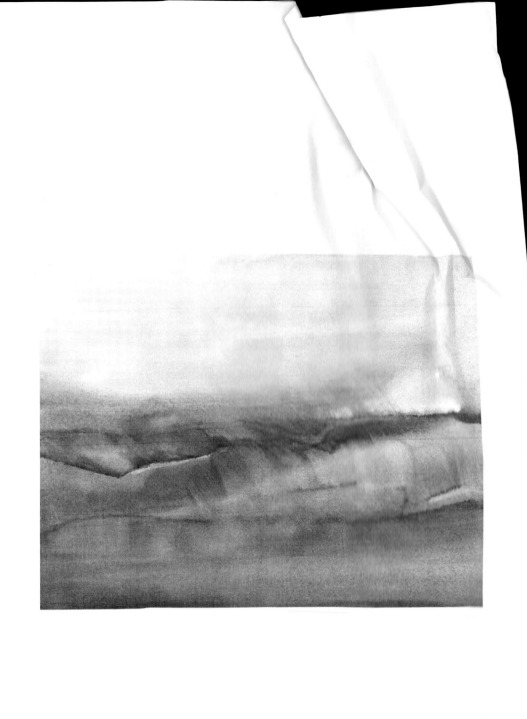

Edwards Brothers Malloy
Thorofare, NJ USA
February 19, 2015